We Never Say Goodbye!

By Jennifer M Maddy

We Never Say Goodbye!

This book was first published in Great Britain in paperback during November 2020.

The moral right of Jennifer M Maddy is to be identified as the author of this work and has been asserted by her in accordance with the Copyright, Designs and Patents Act of 1988.

ISBN-13: 9798572707779

Dedicated to my children
Ben and Leanne Sullivan

CONTENTS

Page

About the Author

Jennifer Maddy is a Qualified Reiki Grand Master, IET (Integrated Energy Therapy) Master, Practitioner & Teacher.

She is also qualified as a Psychic Surgeon. Her Gift as a Light Worker is to "Share her Love & Light" and guide and mentor Souls to connect to the Divine Wisdom WITHIN on their Spiritual Journey to Enlightenment.

Jennifer currently has her own Holistic Spiritual Practice.

She lives in Barleyfield Kilcurry, Dundalk, Co Louth. Ireland.

Jennifer currently works as an Inclusion Classroom Assistant in St. Louis Secondary School, Dundalk.

This is Jennifer's second book, her first, 'Timeless Love' has been well acclaimed, with numerous 5 star reviews on Amazon.

Acknowledgements

I wish to express my sincere and heartfelt appreciation to the testimonies from the wonderful soul friends who contributed to my book. Thank you for listening to your own intuitive guidance and truths from your hearts and sharing intimate stories to inspire the readers to Believe in a great divinity. I am so grateful and overjoyed to unite these stories to ignite Faith.

Don Hale OBE and Dr Steve Green for their contributions.

Thank you Spirit, for this amazing Gift. Thank you to Higher Beings of Light, Guardian Angels, Angels, Archangels, Angels, Ancestors, and Spirit Guides who Guide, Direct, Surround Protect and Structure us all on our Journey, showering us with so many heavenly blessings of Abundance, Bounty and Unconditional Love.

And Finally thank you to my late mum Teresa Maddy for holding the Light.

Please integrate the energy of "Letting Go, Letting God" into your Daily Lives and remember to have patience. All in Divine Timing. One Day at a Time!

Reviews

'Another beautiful contribution to Spiritual Literature from the Divinely guided pen of Jennifer, following on from her first publication, 'Timeless Love', in which she opened up her heart to us about her personal struggles and what brought her to the beautiful place she is now in. Here in this book, we have true stories of inspiration, each one written from the heart, and sent out to us with Love. True stories of how each contributor has made their own connection with All That Is, with the One Great Universal Energy we call God.

Connecting with Spirit, working with the Angelic forces, spreading Love and Light around our beloved Planet Earth, stepping into our own truth and integrity, - it's all here in this beautiful book!'

Eileen McCourt

Reiki Grand Master, Spiritual author and teacher.
www.celestialhealing8.co.uk

"Never Say Goodbye" is such a beautiful book, so full of Angelic Energy in every sentence. When you believe in Angels like I have done for so long, this book ignites the passion for life and huge gratitude for how I have been guided and protected all through my life.

I had the great privilege of knowing Teresa, Jennifer and Andrew's mum. I could see her warm smile in every page.

Thanking Jennifer for allowing me here in this special place.

Kathleen

The widely used saying that 'when the student is ready, the teacher will appear' is the overriding feeling that I got when I read Jennifer Maddy's second book 'We never say goodbye'. The testimonies of those wonderful souls included in Jennifer's book shouted out to me from the pages, and made me hear my own guides and divine messengers who have patiently been shouting loudly at me, for some time! Amidst the hustle and bustle of life, and the fears that get in the way of our true senses, Jennifer's second book is a call to spiritual awakening and renewal to a more enriching and fulfilling life. This book will make it impossible for you to ignore the gentle call to your higher self. As Jennifer whispered so beautifully to her beloved mother as she passed over, it truly is time to 'let go and let God!'

Lorraine Quigley

What an overflow of love and hope I felt when reading each person's journey, each one resonated in my heart.

Great strength, courage and such blessings, brought together by Jennifer in a creative collection

The light of these stories brought light into my heart like a fountain of amazing grace, God's Grace.

Words of such truth, now shared with the world. We never say goodbye to our real truth and beauty, it can sometimes just be forgotten, and then a story is shared and it reminds us.

So, with love and great gratitude I want to thank you all from my heart in coming together, and reminding me.

Karen Binks

Foreword

We are all One, unified in the One Great Universal Energy, the One Great Universal Consciousness we call God. We have no place to possibly exist outside of this Great One Universal Energy. We are the One Great Universal Energy in physical manifestation, - the One Great Universal Energy expressing itself and experiencing itself.

Energy is a vibration frequency. Energy never dies. It cannot be killed, it cannot be ended. Energy is constantly changing, taking new forms and shapes, - that is its essential, basic and fundamental nature. We are energy. And as such, we can never die, we can never end. And the only difference between us all is the energy level frequency on which each one of us is vibrating at any given point in time.

Each of us is an eternal stream of consciousness, infinite awareness, a multi-dimensional, inter-galactic being travelling beyond time and space. We go on forever, just changing energy forms, coming and going throughout the entirety of Creation, in the infinite vastness of eternal Love. God is Love. We are of the God Essence, - we are Love.

And we are all connected in the infinity of that Love. We are all One, but each of us is unique within that Oneness, - unity in diversity. Each one of us is the Great Universal Energy experiencing itself through its own creation.

And in that Oneness, in that connectedness to All That Is, there is constant communication going on between all the various and multitudinous levels of energy that make up the entirety of Creation. Signs being passed constantly, telling us we are never alone, there is no need to fear, we are so greatly loved, we are being looked after in a loving Universe that knows all our needs and is delivering everything that serves our highest good.

William Percy French 1854-1920, was one of Ireland's literary all-time greats. Song writer, musician, poet, artist, all-round entertainer, he travelled the country and abroad, performing and entertaining, from the big houses and royal establishments to the smaller halls in rural Ireland. Percy's first wife, Ettie, died at the tender young age of nineteen from septicaemia in child birth, and their baby daughter followed her just a few weeks later. Percy was deeply Spiritual, deeply connected to All That Is, knowing that death is not the end. '*Only Goodnight*' is the poem he wrote on the passing of his beloved Ettie:

"Only 'goodnight' sweet heart, / And not farewell, / Though for all times thou art / Where angels dwell. / Though for a time those eyes / Lose their soft light,/ Let there be no good-byes, / Only goodnight. / Though for a time they toll / Thy passing bell,/ Tis but 'goodnight', sweet soul,/ And not farewell./ O'er thy sweet lips I sigh - / Lips cold and white / There! - that is not good-bye. / Only 'goodnight'."

There are no goodbyes! There is no end! We simply change

energy form. Just like the caterpillar and the butterfly. Nor do we go away anywhere. Just like the television channels, when we are tuned into one particular channel, all the other channels are still around us, - they have not gone away anywhere.

And there are so many ways for us to connect with the higher energies, the higher beings of Light and our loved ones who have passed before us. One thing is for sure! - They are constantly sending us messages! All we have to do is open up to them!

This beautiful and soul-reaching book is a collection of true and inspirational stories, each written from the heart with Love. Many of the writers I know personally, - from attending my courses and workshops, and from their work as Reiki and other holistic therapists. Each and every one of them is operating on a high energy vibration frequency, deeply connected to Spirit and with a deep awareness and understanding of All That Is. Each and every one is an amazing Lightworker, devoted to helping people to awaken and to make their own Spiritual connection. Each and every one is living life cocooned in, and surrounded by, the Love of higher beings of Light, and each and every one is contributing massively to the huge spiritual awakening process that is going on all around us at this point in earthly time.

Jennifer herself begins by sharing with us the intimate details of her own mother's passing and the beautiful sign she and her brother were given as her mother's Spirit was released and wafted from her body in a surge of neverending, infinite, unconditional Love. And what Jennifer has done by producing this book, is to give all the contributors a chance to tell their own personal story of how each found their own connection, the signs they were given, the synchronicities that led them forward, and how their lives have been impacted through the presence of the angels and the higher beings of Light.

This is a beautiful book. A book about the embodiment of love. A book about opening up to the presence of Spirit in our lives. A book that teaches us many valuable lessons, as learned by those who have written their stories here. Lessons about sacred oneness, respect, nature, acceptance, gratitude, truth, love and compassion.

A book that teaches us that we never say goodbye, for we know that passing from this physical earth energy dimension level is not the end. It is a joyous birthing back again into Spirit, from whence we have all come, and to where we are all returning.

Sending you all Love and Light!

Eileen McCourt - Reiki Grand Master, Spiritual author and teacher.

www.celestialhealing8.co.uk

Pyramid

11th January 2020

A New Year. Setting new Intentions and goals for the year ahead, as I do every year, I held a workshop. IET (integrated energy therapy) Healing with Angels. My friend Brenda Murnaghan joined me with her Sound Bath. Sacred Sound. Tools emitting a sound frequency. As the class gets under way, we write down our intentions for the year with our students, a bit like a vision board. It is Sacred HEALING as we invite universal energy to work with us, merging together in a Group setting, enhances the energy and intention for each person as we unite in unity. I personally set the intention to write this book, and so it is.

Please enjoy the True Stories shared by genuine people. Thank you to each one for contributing. The word Holistic is an adjective that describes treating the whole person characterized by the belief that the parts of something are intimately interconnected. By exploring different people's experiences and perceptions we can relate to our own beliefs and innate knowing opening up the gateway to our own minds and Spiritual Consciousness (conscience) awareness. Being part of a greater collective awakening and the embodiment of LOVE. Trust your VIBES.

In early March I had a DREAM. In the dream I was lying under A Meditation Pyramid (A Divine Sacred Geometric

Design) designed in order to bring about an alignment of the planet and our spiritual abilities. Everything is locked into geometric form, to divine sound, and the colours of the rays of light that comes from within. As a human being, even a tree or a flower, everything is based upon this design. It is the nature of God. Inside this temple, your telepathy of love and the quieting of the mind and connection between you and God in previous lives becomes awakened. Amazingly, this dream came through and became my reality.

The intention is to help as many people as possible to awaken. The Pyramid was placed in my Healing Cabin. This sacred tool magnifies and amplifies CRYSTAL CLEAR intentions. It is magnetic combining copper and crystals creating a Portal of Unconditional Love. This became a time of study and growth, as I gained knowledge and wisdom reading, meditating and connecting within. I feel so honoured to be able to Share this Healing Modality now with people.

Heather from MindSoul (a holistic service) invited me to go online every week and deliver a meditation/guidance live from Facebook blog. I was very nervous at first but after a few weeks, I fell into this role and now I enjoy sharing my insight into words, our language that we speak to ourselves on a daily basis and how it can affect us . Change your thoughts, change your mind. We are like a magnet and in the law of attraction we attract to us what we believe and feel inside.

I personally invite Angels and Higher Vibrations of Light to work with me. Angels are thoughts of God who love for the sake of loving and exist through service to Grace. They are non-gender, non-judgmental holy orbs of light. The Angels inspire us to proclaim the same acts of heart felt love, using the gift of alchemy for trans mutational healing, pranic upliftment and spiritual empowerment. We are a reflection of this Grace.

Inviting the Angels into your life is a beautiful Gift. They help create structure. They give clear guidance. I never doubted their messages and trusted their wisdom as they opened doorways and led me to the right people to share their stories. They have the Gift of Excellence.

Currently we are moving through a time of accelerated evolution into the Golden Age of Aquarius. Experiencing this shift of transformation can be challenging. Cancel, Clear and Delete old stagnant Thought Programmes and repeated patterns of outdated behaviours is necessary to reset and come into alignment with our own Source Light Energy. (our minds are like a computer). Through this book and its inspiration true-life stories shared by genuine heartfelt people, I invite the reader to have an open mind, free of judgement stepping into their own truth and integrity. I integrate some of our traditions from our Ancestors, Spirit Guides and Higher Beings of Light and include messages from Spirit including my own mum Teresa Maddy, whom I dedicate this book to.

We will work through your chakra system from you Soul Star (god essence) to your Earth Star (mother essence) and merge this Love in your Heart Star (Divine Duel essence) to become a conduit of Love and Light embracing your Shadow. I invite you to have a Blank Canvas and a Clean Slate of Awareness. Please enjoy.

Today is the 11th of November 2020. A huge portal of Love has opened. I feel honoured and blessed to be alive at this Time and grateful. Please read my first book" Timeless Love" where I shared my own journey through my own Spiritual Awakening a few years ago.

NOW. Let US unite in prayer, gratitude, reverence, sacred oneness, sovereignty, truth love and compassion in this Lifetime. Let us teach our children Morals of GRACE, RESPECT AND LOVE and ground this energy into our Planet through Mother EARTH.

Silence

ANGELIC NUMBER 222

Trust that everything is working out exactly as it's supposed to be, with Divine Blessings for everyone involved.

AS MY BELOVED MUM GENTLY TOOK HER FINAL BREATH, I WHISPERED THE WORDS IN HER EAR.

Let Go, Let God. Let Go, Let God, Let Go, Let God.

I looked over at my brother Andrew. A sensation of peace washed over us as our eyes connected. The three of us were holding hands. A feeling of relief and Joy filled our bodies, as we released our beloved mum Teresa Maddy back to Spirit. She was gone.

"Do you believe me now?", I whispered to my brother. No, he replied and stood up. I looked at him in sheer amazement.

Moments before, as our beloved mums' breath was slowing, her old Nokia phone placed on the bedside locker table beeped. I had lifted the phone over to see who it was and to my disbelief the number 2 appeared on the screen. "what does that mean", my brother asked. In Spiritual terms, I replied the number 2 means,

Let go, let God.

I looked at my mum in wonder. During her last breath on this Earthly Plane, she had gifted me with a spiritual blessing. The Biggest Gift of Faith. Faith that we are larger than the eyes can see. Faith that our Spirit never dies. It transcends all time and space into the vastness of eternal love. Faith that "We never Say Goodbye"

We hold the key in our Hearts Forever.

SONG; *HAIL MARY - GENTLE WOMAN* by *John Rodgers*.

"Gentle Mother, Quiet Light,

Morning Star, so strong and Bright,

Gentle Mother, Peaceful Dove,

Teach us Wisdom,

Teach us LOVE"

As I sit in my little wooden cabin, in my back garden, the light of the sun is shining its bright golden rays through the windows. My wind chimes of Blue Lace Agate ring gently in the breeze, bringing a peace and calmness to my mind. The door of the Cabin is slightly open welcoming in fresh air as the breeze blows in around my papers. Scribbles, scribbles, scribbles on pages everywhere. I am constantly writing notes on sheets, allowing the words to flow like water.

Angel Cards surround me, with delightful messages and pictures. A little Compass in the middle of the table navigating my pen on the paper as I begin writing this Book. I have invited my Spirit Guides to help and I envision a Victorian Setting from a past life that I have lived, as the knowledge and wisdom is revealed.

My little dogs play outside separated from the chickens and rabbits that my daughter adores, and my son silently loves, enjoying the magic of nature. They have not a care or concern in the world. Oh, how as children we also felt this energy of childlike innocence. Not worrying about life. living in the moment. Sometimes as life gets in the way, we forget that deep inside us we are Diamonds, Pristine, Flawless, Radiant Brilliant and Fabulous. Crystal Clear.

DO YOU BELIEVE IN MAGIC?

I DO!!!!!!

Mother Bear Lucy

Lucy has guided and protected me on my journey through Good and Bad Times over the last decade. I trust and confide in her. She never judges my actions but helps me evolve and grow. Grow to Glow, or Glow to Grow. Lucy was one of my first students to be attuned in Basic, Intermediate and Advanced levels of IET (integrated energy therapy). Her connection with Arch Angel Ariel and Spirit is Heartfelt and True.

Archangel Ariel

Archangel Ariel is the Goddess of marriage and childbirth. The Name Ariel means 'Lion of God' and as Jennifer is a Leo, I am not at all surprised that she asked me to write a little on this particular Angel for her book!

Ariel is also Hebrew for bravery and courage which Jen has always shown immense bravery and courage throughout her own story as you know from reading her first book, Timeless Love.

In the Hebrew Bible Ariel is one of the names used for the city Jerusalem and the temple where Jesus would have travelled for the Passover three maybe four times, this is where he also spoke with great knowledge to the scholars and holy men at age twelve standing in his power and truth at such a young age.

Now we know AA Ariel as the Angel of Nature. She protects mother nature, the animals, birds and plants and also supervises the care of the elements, EARTH, FIRE, WIND and AIR. Ariel also helps us humans figure out how to live to our full potential, to live in our own truth with courage and confidence and that we have all the tools we require to fulfil Gods purpose for us. She can help us get organised and set clear goals for achieving what it is we want to achieve in life. She is a wonderful help to get us over obstacles we may face while trying to reach our goals. As the Angel of Courage, she helps us transcend our worries and fears and helps open our minds to new ways of getting through confused or dark times. Using your intention, your imagination, your thoughts, connect to Ariel and ask her to help you with your endeavors don't dwell on it, just carry on and as if by magic you will see what it is you are looking for or be inspired with an idea to overcome an obstacle or meet the person you have been waiting for.

One of the crystals which resonates at the same frequency as Ariel is Rose Quartz it is a great tool for reminding us to love ourselves first and then when your cup overflows with self-love to pour that love out into the world in our relationships and work all the while coming back to the self to checking and refill one's own cup as we move through life. Keeping a piece of this crystal on you may help your own vibration shift into a higher frequency of understanding or may just remind us to think through our problems using love instead of fear.

Pink is Ariel's colour so you may see the colour pink, or pink light or pink flowers often when working with Ariel. One of the tools I use if I am feeling anxious or not in my full power , is to surround myself in a ball of pink light, something like the good witch in the Wizard of Oz movie, and I allow myself to believe that I am safe and protected and that I can move through life protected and strong , even while experiencing difficulties. The colour pink can remind us that we can believe to see and understand events in a different way and not to be overpowered or left feeling helpless by them. It sounds so simple, but a powerful technique that can help get you through the toughest times.

As Ariel helps with earthly manifestation, she will also help with unblocking the flow of abundance in your life. Here is a short invocation to ask for her help:

AA Ariel please align my vibrations with the divine gifts of abundance and prosperity please clear all blocks to my financial security Please allow abundance to flow my way I give all worries fears and doubts over to my Angels and so it is with God's blessing.

AA Ariel is a motherly energy comforting, kind and soft yet strong and fierce when necessary. Enjoy working with her she will protect you like a mother lion protects her cubs.

Love Lucy xxx

Cherub Angel

I started my life like many others with hopes, dreams and aspirations for my future. Somewhere along the road of my life, those dreams vanished and I took many dark roads through my choices, actions and negative mindset. During one of these dark periods, I was alone, afraid and on the brink of insanity. That night I internally pleaded for help, and it arrived. A friend of mine had passed away tragically and I had not had contact with his mother for quite some years, a woman of great faith, I might add. This lady rapped my window, walked into my home and told me to pack my bags. She said I was going to stay with her. This lady saved my life that night. I am under no illusions that the Angels orchestrated this line of event and had heard and answered my internal prayers.

A number of years later while I was involved with a national worldwide group of evolved people, I was asked to investigate and examine my beliefs of a higher power. Opening my mind. One particular night I met with a friend to discuss this topic at length and we shared our ideas. The question of a Higher power weighed heavy on my mind. I dug deep inside looking for answers. We decided to go to a Sound Bath. For anyone who has never gone to a Sound Bath before this is a high vibrational healing portal of sound which creates a higher frequency of awareness. I set the intention "if there is something out there, please make yourself known vividly. See this was a whole new world for me. I'd journeyed through the depts of despair, lost myself, lost everything. Now I was taking action and attending positive new healing events to help gain a higher perspective. I went home from the Sound Bath and while my family were asleep, I was searching through spiritual programs on the TV. Out of the corner of my eye, I saw a Golden Light. In the centre of this Golden Light was a cherub angel, floating mid-air. I kept looking away disbelieving, questioning my mind. Three times I looked and looked away still disbelieving what I was witnessing. Only earlier that same day, I had set the intention for answers and now my mind would not allow me to believe what I was seeing. I had asked for a sign and I got it. I can honestly put my hand on my heart and say with conviction, that what I saw was real. We are always supported on our journey, if we ask, believe and receive.

During this time, I had been receiving Angelic Healing treatments and learning IET (integrated energy therapy) healing with Angels with Jennifer and my whole world changed. Today I am blessed to have been attuned to this Healing Modality and I have a healing practice now myself. Who would have believed where my journey had started. This is now my souls' path. I feel confident and love being authentically myself in this area of work, where before I was always afraid of what other people thought of me, judging myself through other people's eyes, which is a self-disastrous trait. I have been saved so many times in my life from dangerous situations on my path. Some might say this story is a coincidence. I don't believe that.

Angels have been guiding and protecting me all along, I just had to learn how to invite them into my life to work with me. I was never alone. I have learned information that mentioned that cherubs are part of the angelic realm. They most definitely are. I've seen one!

Love Stephanie (Healing Angels) xxx

Picture by David Connor, his orb of light, that guides him.

My Pal Lisa

As I sit here starting to write this I realise three things:

1.It is Friday 13th - a date feared by many but over the last few years I have since discovered that Friday the 13th is actually the day of the Great Goddess, a day to worship the divine feminine that lives in us all. It was considered a powerful day to manifest, honour creativity and to celebrate the beauty, wisdom and nourishment of the soul. If you have never heard about this go check it out, you will be amazed.

2.This Friday 13th coincidentally falls the same week, just two days after 11/11, another huge day for manifestation - go check that out too if you don't already know about it.

3.It is exactly 10 years this weekend since I met the lovely Jennifer. We met on a Ki Massage course in Dublin yet we soon discovered we had grown up in the same parish and I was very soon to be moving to just round the corner from her childhood home (where she now lives again). We became friends straight away. Jennifer looked very different back then, her hair was still short after her coming through her cancer treatment, I loved it, she didn't love it quite so much and couldn't wait for it to grow back!! Jen came across initially as shy and quiet but looking back now I can see that she was probably just finding her feet in her new spiritual world. In those 10 years Jen has continued to face her fears with strength and courage. Her light, which had started off so small could now fill a room and beyond, never mind her infectious laugh!

Those ten-years have led us on very separate paths. Jennifer's children were teenagers then, I had a one year old at the time and then two years later had another baby. My journey with Ki massage has stopped and started so many times but Jen has always been there cheering me on no matter where life took me. We have gone very long periods of time with not being in contact but when we do connect it's like nothing has changed. Jen sees the light in me and has always encouraged me to allow it to shine bright. I've been on a journey of my own over those ten-years with all sorts thrown in, post-natal depression, having a baby who was deemed failure to thrive, a child who was diagnosed with a neurological condition, financial issues, a melanoma scare, LIFE in general! I have learned so much over those years, about myself and about the world around me. No matter how many times I feel like a failure for not using my talents Jen always reassures me that my time has not been right, and it hasn't, but, my day will come and it will be sooner rather than later.

Angels have been part of my life for as long as I can remember, from the prayer we all learned "Oh Angel of God, my guardian dear...." to Mammy telling me everyone has a guardian angel looking out for them.

My granny was a very spiritual lady, and she was way ahead of here time, meditating, reading spiritual books, challenging certain people and situations and wearing the colour purple - lots! She gave me my first set of angel cards, way back in the day when an angel card consisted of just one word! No beautiful illustrations to go with it, but they were every bit as powerful.

My granny died suddenly while myself and Mammy were away on holidays. I will never forget when I got to the house from the airport, I went out to sit on the step and this black cat appeared out of nowhere. I'll not say I hate cats but let's just say I had no particular love for them. Well this cat would not leave me be - to this day I believe that was Clora coming to comfort me and say goodbye. The very first time I visited my grandfather after the funeral the same cat appeared at the door.

Many years after, during a very emotional shamanic healing journey with Shane Donohue, a message came through that a part of me had died that day and that Granny was now telling me to not be sad and go and live my life. On the way home from that session a black cat ran across the road in front of me.

This is just one example of how I have always been aware of signs and synchronicities. There are many more and I have no doubt that one day I will have enough of a story to sit and write my very own book.

For now, I applaud Jennifer for writing hers, I thank her

for asking me to contribute and I also thank her for always being there in the side lines encouraging me to grow, just like she has done.

Wishing whoever is reading this right now, much love, light and hope xx

"Do the best you can until you know better. Then, when you know better, do better"- Maya Angelou.

Love Lisa xxx

Divine Lights; Henry and Heidi

Anyone that is in a similar situation than me is not alone. There is help out there and they will get through it! Looking after yourself is very important, especially when you have little empaths picking up on your energy. If it is good, it will ripple out to them. I will always be here for anyone that is going through a spiritual challenge with their children.

I know we as parents believe our children are special, and we have every right to believe this because our children are so special and unique. None of them are the same and I would like to share why both of my children are a certain kind of special...

I am married to David, the most caring and supportive husband in the world and we have two super amazing children, Henry (6) and Heidi (4) Some might call them 'Crystal Children', 'Indigo Children' or 'Earth Angels'...I'm not really one for labels but in some cases I feel it can be beneficial...

When I was pregnant with Henry I felt he was different. I always felt different as a child myself but this particular feeling I had was very intense. I connected so deeply to him. I found myself telling my close family that this baby was going to be special and how he was going to be a gifted healer. I just knew!

When Henry was born, he looked like such an old soul and everyone I met said as much! From he was almost four months old he would go into trances. You could actually see him reading your soul with his piercing blue eyed. From no age he would tell me he could see spirit, but he could also see the scary things. And I mean very scary! He barely slept. He was constantly scared. This was so unbelievably hard to witness.

I know I have had tremendous support from my family, in particular, my mum and dad and brother, Shane, but I still felt so alone!

When Henry turned one, I knew I needed some extra support so I decided to take him out to see a wonderful healer, Martin. Martin has supported me over the years, and I thank God every day for his help. He has taken me on quite the journey. He has led me to a place of calm and has helped me gain the strength and confidence I needed, not just as a mother but as a guide. I was full of self-doubt, but he reminded me that I am light and have plenty of it. I am now at a point in my life where I feel more than capable of coping with all of life's challenges...

By using my light and trusting myself it has helped me help my children on so many levels. Henry is such a remarkable young boy and is able to handle this gift so much more not. He is much more grounded and has such a natural talent when it comes to dealing with animals, tuning forks and crystals. He feels at home with himself when he hosts a healing session. He melts my heart beyond words.

As for little Heidi.

She is also a gifted Healer and a very special wee soul. The joy she brings to us every day is just incredible. I have such a beautiful connection with her and I just love when our eyes lock into one another's. She has the most unusual voice and when she sings, our hearts just beam with love and pride. She has seen Angels and felt presences around her...not as intense as her brother but the gift is there, for sure!

When Heidi is around animals it is the most beautiful sight... we call her 'the animal whisperer'. She has a magic touch around animals and is at her happiest when she is around her dog, Poppy.

Almost three years ago, Poppy got run over by a lorry. There wasn't much hope for her. She was in pretty bad shape and the vet suggested putting her down! We were devastated to hear this but we didn't feel it was the right decision to make. She made it through an operation, and we got her home. The children made banners and blew up balloons for her arrival. Poppy actually cried when she saw the children. It was such a touching moment. She wasn't able to walk for a couple of months, but the love and support Henry and Heidi gave her was incredible. They suggested doing "Minion Healing" on her. Every day we gave her healing and my word she felt it! We feel so blessed to still have our wee Poppy with us and the children often remind her of how we healed her!

When you tell people that your children can see spirit or can heal animals it can make some feel rather uncomfortable and actually avoid you and that's ok. I am proud of my children and their gifts!

I have taught my children that they are born with the most amazing divine light and when someone bully's us or upsets us our light can get dimmed...They are still very young but they know how important it is to keep their light shining bright and not to dim anyone else's.

It is so important for me to be around like-minded people and I feel so unbelievably lucky and blessed to have our children in the most wonderful school with a very empathic principal, Mairéad Egan. Mairéad has the most beautiful soul and shines from the inside out! She has no idea how much she has helped me...When we were in a very challenging situation with Henry, she never once judged us and that meant the absolute world to us. She could see this ability as a gift and was very mindful about it all. I feel so at ease knowing that such a beautiful Lightworker looks out for all of our children in our wee community.

I am honoured to know you Jennifer, and really appreciate all I have learned and continue to learn from you. You are a true an inspiration!

Thank you for writing this beautiful book and for giving me the opportunity to openly talk about some of the most precious gifts in my life.

Much love and light,

Love Laura xxx

Archangels

MICHAEL, RAPHAEL, GABRIEL AND URIEL

My daughter was 18 years old and studying in Toronto for a year. She was apartment hunting so I flew out to join her. We booked into a hotel for the week and because time was limited she stayed up late every night checking what was available. We were not having much luck and time was running out so settling down to sleep one night I asked the Archangels for help. I said "Archangel Michael, Raphael, Gabriel and Uriel could you please fly along Bloor Street and find my daughter a safe and suitable place to live". No sooner was visualisation complete when I heard "Mum, are you awake? I think I might have found a place… " I knew that was the one, so she booked a viewing for the next day. The Archangels had found it! I thanked them and we both enjoyed a proper sleep that night.

The following day we saw the apartment and it was perfect! It wasn't available for five days and I was flying home in two days' time, so I booked her into a small family run hotel near the new apartment. I was concerned about that, it felt strange, but I had to trust that she would be alright. I boarded the bus to the airport and asked Archangel Michael to take care of her and if at all possible to do something to allow me to stay a few more days. We sat on the plane for a very long time, so I asked a steward what was happening. He said there was a problem with one of the engines. Archangel Michael was at work!! We disembarked and I was sent back to my daughter in an Airport limousine with a voucher to call one when I wanted to fly home! We spent a wonderful few days together shopping for things for her new place and enjoying nice meals. She settled in, I said my goodbyes and left in my Airport limo! I felt blessed. My prayer every day since is... "Thank you Archangels for hearing our call for help, coming to our aid and bringing your wonderful miracles into our lives.

POEM *BY MAURA*

Angels of Heaven, Angels of God.

Thank you for filling our lives, full of Love, Peace, Happiness and Blessings. And Light, Bright, Angelic Energy. Night and Day.

Later in the book you will read True inspiration stories explaining how Archangels Raphael, Gabriel and Michael have influenced other people's lives too.

Archangel Uriel

She/He represents, The Flame of the Lord or " Light of GOD.

AFFIRMATION:

I call upon you now, to stand by me.

Please remove all emotional fears and blocks.

Please crown me with your Divine Light.

Please fill me with Love, Serenity and Confidence.

Love Maura xxx

Archangels Gabriel and Raphael

Archangel Gabriel is my go-to Angel. I was introduced to him by a saintly nun called Sister Angela, who prepared me and my seven-year old classmates for First Holy Communion. She must have been a very wise teacher because even at seven, we were not afraid to know there was an Angel sent by God to each of us on the day we were born and that angel would protect and inspire and keep us safe all of our lives. My little group of friends names ours and although we were all girls, we called them men's saint names. I choose Gabriel. And hand on my heart he has never let me down. If I didn't get what I heavenly prayed for, he sent me the consolation needed to bear the disappointment and pain. I am in my 70's now and all through my life I've been blessed knowing I only had to say the Angel of God, My Guardian Angel Prayer and everything would be easier.

I even pray to my children's guardian Angels for them..... Angel of God, His/hers Guardian Dear and I am sure it helps them even though I wouldn't tell them.

Meditation is very popular and Beneficial now, but my meditation time is when I go for a daily walk and pray to St Gabriel and admire and enjoy nature. I get great comfort from it and St Gabriel never got tired and give up on me.

Angel of God, my Guardian Dear,

To Whom God's Love commits me here,

Ever this day (or night) be at my side,

To Light and Guard,

To Rule and Guide.

Amen.

October 2nd is Feast of our Guardian Angels.

Angel Gabriel is the Messenger of God. His message to us is to connect with the flow of the universe with God's breath. Angel Gabriel wishes us to be influenced by the Divine and allow true Inspiration to flow. Thereby you will protect the exquisite vulnerability of your soul's truth. He helps us with Divine Direction and Trusting the flow of Life.

Love Eileen Connolly xxx

I call on Saint Raphael to help lift my head, so that I may be guided into the Light. To help with the suffering from the Past. The hurt and pain made me fall. I struggled to lift my head at all. I wanted to wave my clear white flag.

I then connected to Saint Raphael who brightened my path on my journey to Healing and guided me to pull back my white flag.

Poem written by Caitlin Flynn, *6th year Student from St. Louis Secondary School.*

Caitlin is visually impaired. She had a tumour at the very young age of 10 years of age. While in hospital recovering, Caitlin was in a ward called RAPHAEL. Caitlin took this name for her confirmation. I have no doubt that Raphael guides her, she is truly inspirational, and we will miss you when you finish secondary school. Please remember "We never say goodbye". Love Jen.

St. Raphael. God has healed.

Opening up to Angels

It was in the summer of 2018, when my life started to change. My second child Lucas was less than one-year old and was a handful, I was feeling exhausted a good proportion of the time, I had a good few other challenges in my life. That summer, I decided I needed to start healing, so I made a concerted effort to use what limited spare time I had to do just that. I practiced Pilates, received three sessions of pranic healing, learned some tai chi, experienced a sound bath for the first time, meditated frequently. On the night of Tuesday 31st July 2018, I felt tingles above my head, I am now very familiar with these sensations, it was my Angels letting me know they were there for me, all I had to do was ask for help. On that same day, they also showed me visible signs – namely dropping white feathers in my path. I was getting more and more sensitive by the day.

I knew I had a calling; I just didn't know what it was. I opened up a little more each day. Life got in the way sometimes or perhaps life through its difficulties and subsequent lessons, it showed me the way.

In late 2018, I received a clearing consultation/phone call, which looking back now I know helped clear old patterns and make way for new possibilities. Early 2019, I received a deep Shirodhara facial Treatment to help open up my third eye and this led me to finding the beginning of my true path and meeting the lovely Jennifer Maddy. I had no idea what Integrated Energy Therapy was or what the 'Healing Angels of the Energy Field' workshop would entail, but I was sure it was me, I was guided by my intuition – the Angels led me to Jen's very capable, gifted hands.

Jen explained that day would be about inviting the nine IET Angels into my life. She had a beautiful poster on the wall, with pictures of the Angels. I was especially drawn to Archangel Michael, as I knew he had been helping me by blessing me with strength and integrity. And then when Jen told me about Angel Sarah and how her gifts of empowerment can help you overcome obstacles in your life, I was so glad I had trusted myself and took this extra step to work with the Angels.

Jen made me feel right at home, she has a vibrant essence and soft energy and is totally trusting of our Angels and the guidance they give us. This inspired me. I felt so relaxed and at peace when she gave me a an IET healing treatment. When I was receiving the initiation, I felt very clearly three drops pour on to my forehead. My eyes were closed and afterwards I asked Jen if she had poured water or oil on me, her answer was no. And so, that solidified my belief in Angels and the higher beings of light.

I have since went on to learn the Basic, Intermediate and advanced levels of IET with Jen to help me fully realise my soul mission! My path with the Angels has led me to attune, practice and teach Rahanni Celestial healing, I also offer intuitive Angel Card readings and one to one or group meditations. People that receive healing have all sorts of different experiences, they see visions, feel sensations, sometimes hear messages, feel incredibly relaxed, comforted and peaceful. It's a heaven on earth type of experience.

My spiritual gifts, intuition and sensitivity are developing. What a journey this has been so far! We have set up a family business selling AUREAL Candles, handmade with Love using our combined creative gifts. The word Aureal means Aura Heal.

I have witnessed the beautiful ripple effect of working with the Angels and practicing Angelic healing. My nine-year-old daughter, Maggie has opened up greatly, where once she would have been quite anxious, she is now much more accepting of life and deals with her feelings in a very intuitive and emotionally intelligent way. Together we learned a meditation to meet your Guardian Angel, she speaks clearly of her Angels, their names and asks them directly for help. We very much work as a team, I learn from her as much as she learns from me or maybe more so!

Maggie's Angel

Love Deirdre xxx

Faith

Looking back reminiscing over the years since my childhood, growing up in a devout Catholic family, the Rosary Prayer was a great part of our daily lives and the faith that was instilled in us from our parents.

I was always aware of my Faith and the importance of God the Father and our Mother Mary in my life. From an early age of six years, I always visualised, God the father, walking with me, holding my hand, talking to me and telling me" not to be afraid". God felt like my only friend, someone I could trust and confide in, when I felt alone and unsure of this life, and what the future would hold. "Footprints in the Sand."

During my life there have sadly been moments and phrases when I said "God, I cannot do this, please give me strength and courage to live"

One day, I was in a Strandfield in Dundalk with my friend Jennifer. On the wall I noticed a beautiful Holy Cross, which stood out. I felt very drawn to this amazing cross. My Soul danced with Joy and I knew I had to buy it. My life has changed vastly since that day. My Beautiful Cross has the gift of Motherhood and other blessings. My life has now a new fundamental meaning. It has always been my faith that carried me through.

'The healing Angels of the Energy Field' by Stevan J Thayer.

"Angel Faith's Gift. There is the need for Faith in Something bigger than myself who knows what is really going on in my life. Faith that there really is a divinity who loves me personally and wants the best for me.

Like the Footprints in the Sand Poem .... even when I can't go on, this Divinity picks me up and carries me".

Love Dymphna xx

Karl was adopted just like me in the early 70's. Unfortunately, Karl lost oxygen during his birth for a few minutes and was born with special needs. He was adopted into a very loving home in Dublin and had a happy childhood.

Unfortunately, both his brothers from this family had muscular dystrophy problems. They both died at a young age. His adopted Dad passed away too, leaving Karl with his mother Peggy O'Kelly.

Karl has been a God sent to Peggy. He is her treasure, as she is his. Where would they be in life without this love and support. This story confirms that there is a greater divinity and picture for our lives, even if we can't see it for ourselves.

Karl is highly thought of by the Adopted Community. He is an advocate for people who are adopted. We are all Crib Mates on this journey of Life.

Love Karl xxx

Faith Healers

When I started on my Journey on discovery to Healing, I kept hearing the name Michael McBride mentioned. When we sometimes hear the same thing repeated 3 times, it's a Sign. Take notice. I decided to call to see this Man. My friend Brenda came with me. We sat on the wall outside his home waiting for Michael to appear. In the distance, I could hear a car coming, and I intuitively know it was him. "Why are you here" he asked...

This was the start of a valued friendship that would last for our lifetime. Michael and his wife Mary welcomed me into their home. It was a privilege watching Michael heal a child or an adult who had chickenpox or shingles. He would pray and put his hands on the pain. Over the years, I have gained so much knowledge and respect for this Gift. As I write this story, its Michael's wife Mary's second anniversary, as she has passed to spirit. I woke up this morning and she was my first thought. This is my intuition guiding me. Never ignore this feeling or vibe. It's your higher self-showing you the way. Trust your Vibe and take action if you feel it's the Right Action. I am so glad I didn't ignore the Signs that Spirit showed me years ago, I am a better person today from the experience of meeting Michael and Mary. Sending you both so much love and respect.

Love Jen xxx

SONG: CELINE DION (The prayer)

Angels of Unconditional Love

Just a bit of context. I keep a diary and had been writing on it as I was going through some difficult times, my head was, as my GP said, "very muddled up" and I was starting to wonder when I'd come out of the hole.

"I need to write this. I just had the visit of an Angel. Quite literally. No doubt this sounds as if my marbles indeed have been scattered.

I don't think so.

I decided - or just did - to light my candles, lie on the couch, listen to relaxing music. I was facing the mirror where, on the shelf, I have 2 long candles, identical, side by side. On the right corner of the room, above the fireplace, I put another small candle in front the picture of Teresa Maddy and myself.

I started talking to Teresa in my head but couldn't feel her. The long candle on the right, over the shelf, started to flicker and would stop for a while. I was still talking to Teresa but would tell myself I was only speaking to myself as I couldn't feel her with me.

I prayed to her and to Angels to help me.

The same long candle was flickering wildly through this now and I realized that its flame was twice as high as the other one on the left.

I then knew it was my Teresa reaching out to me.

I looked at our picture and was talking to her when I realized that I never put the little candle there. It is part of a set and I always have them together. But tonight, I did not, and the light of the candle was shining brightly straight on the two of us.

I knew she was here of course, always to guide me and help me as she always did. Out of the blue came the idea to ask Jen for a treatment. That didn't come from me. Teresa told me to do that. I know it.

I texted Jen to ask her. I looked back at the candle and I smiled. It had gone back to its normal size, like the other one.

Then came to me that thought. Whenever I had problems, I would talk to Teresa, she would listen and tell me what she thought and when I would leave, she would say to me: "Everything will work out, I'll light a candle for you."

My dearest friend, so heartbreakingly missed, is no longer here with us and yet she is, whenever I want to call out to her, I know she is always here with me. This fills me with so much gratitude and love. As Jen writes this book called. "WE NEVER SAY GOODBYE!"

All my Love,

Caroline. Xxx

A Fable about a Dream.

"Why do we listen to our Hearts, because that is where you'll find your treasure". Keep listening to what it has to say. But my heart is a "traitor" the boy said to the alchemist. "It doesn't want me to go on" "That makes sense".

"Naturally its afraid, that in pursuing your dream you might lose everything you've won.

Then why should I listen to my Heart?

Because you will never again be able to keep it quiet. Even if you pretend not to have heard what it tells you, it will always be there repeating to you what you're thinking about Life and the World. Every second of the Search is an encounter with God.

"When I have been truly searching for my treasure, every day has been luminous, because I've known that every hour was a part of the dream, that I would find it".

That is my Destiny.

Hugging

One evening, I went to collect my son from Adam's house. His mum Geraldine was delighted to see me. She said she had a message from my mum Teresa Maddy in spirit. She sees you sad and hurting, and she wants you to know that she loves you and is always with you. She is handing you a Yellow Sunflower. She wants you to be happy. Geraldine then put her arms around me and put my head on her chest. I could feel my mum's arms around me, small and frail but yet strong and gentle.

I let out a sob as though my heart would break. I had been holding my grief deep inside. Geraldine through her wisdom with Spirit has given my Soul Permission to Let Go. I started to cry and cry and cry. I released so much grief and pain from the sadness of losing my beloved mum. My heart began to feel lighter and brighter.

Thank you Geraldine.

Love Jen xxx

I AM THE LOVE OF GOD, " I AM" Song by Denise Hagan

Connecting with Dominic's Spirit

25th of November 2018

I felt the sudden urge to draw and I had no idea why. Before I knew it, I had drawn a woman wiping her tears saying I'm fine. I had no idea why I drew this picture and give it no energy or thought. Later in March 2019, during an angel online group which I was connected to, a member posted up a picture of her son who had died. Straight away I felt drawn to his eyes and amazed that I was able to speak to her son in spirit Dominic

I immediately got in contact with his mum. Her son told me he was only 19 and that his name was D. He showed me visions on how he had passed through suicide. Later on, talking to his mum, she was able to confirm with me that his name was Dominic and he introduced himself as D to friends. His mum also said that he was 19 when he died, and this confirmed my Vision.

I started to get friendly with his family. I felt like I had to in order to help them. One day Dominic came through to me again saying he wanted his family to make candles in his memory. His family went on to do this and also created a Charity in America in his name called DOMINIC'S LIGHT.

Next Becky (his aunt) as he called her was messaging me asking me what I do in my spare time and of course I said" drawing". She asked to see some of my artwork. For some reason, I felt like I had to show her the drawing I had done in November previous. Her words were "Oh my God, that's Shawn, Dominic's mum". I told her the date of the drawing and she confirmed that was the date Dominic took his own life.

They have told me many times that I have helped them more then they will ever know.

Love Celine McGahon (Soul Sisters) xxx

Celine is from Dundalk, Co Louth. Her connection with DomInic and his family in America is awe inspiring. Dominic communicates his thoughts through Celine. She lights Lanterns of Light on his Anniversary and Birthday in his memory.

SONG by Celine Dion and Bee Gees "We don't say goodbye!" IMMORTALITY

This is a poem written by Caitlin Flynn, a 6th year student from St. Louis Secondary School, Dundalk for a young boy who sadly died in a car accident recently. May his Spirit Rest in Peace in the arms of the Angels.

Your wings are ready, so fly high and far to see the foreboding world you left behind. When you parted, you took my heart, so don't let it fall. Now, it' TIME for your well needed rest and we will as always hold you in the highest respect.

ANCESTORS

Over the last year, I was fortunate to meet James Sweeney. Known as Mystic James 1111. James is originally from America. He has connected to his Ancestors over the past years and this has brought him on quite a journey. On exchanging treatments of Angels and Ancestors, I started to open up more to this Energy. I feel more grounded now and grateful for all . Our Ancestors like our Angels are thrilled when we ask for their help. This is a Native American Lakota Prayer. It holds healing and gratitude for all beings.

Aho, Mitakuye, Oyasin.

All my relatives, I honour you in this circle of life with us today. I am grateful for this opportunity to acknowledge you in prayer. To the creator for the Ultimate Gift of Life.

I thank you.

To the mineral nation, that has built and maintained my Bones and all foundation of Life Experiences.

I thank you.

To the planet nation that sustains my organs and body and gives me healing herbs for sickness.

I thank you.

To the animal nation that feeds me, and offers your local companionship in this walk of life,

I thank you.

To the human nation that shares my paths, a Soul upon the Sacred Wheel of Life

I thank you.

To the Spirit Nation that guides me invisible through the ups and downs of life and for carrying the Torch of Light through the Ages.

I thank you.

In my last book, "Timeless Love," I wrote about my journey to connecting to my birth family. This has been a very rewarding experience and I have grown in so many ways by opening these doors. Feeling so much love. I am a better person now and feel more balanced. I recently completed an Ancestral DNA Kit. This is exciting as I am going to expand my horizons and connect to more people worldwide. The Angels and Ancestors support us on our Journey.

Love Jen xxx

ANGELS OF FORGIVENESS

The art of forgiving. For me it's a lifestyle choice. If I had the choice not to forgive in any situation and harbour the resentment within that comes with choosing not to forgive someone I'd be serving myself and ultimately others a disadvantage. I want to be the brightest person I possibly can, to show others they can too and to do that I need to give myself the best chance. Forgiveness is much more than pride. It's a releasing tool and accepting people are only human. I visual everyone wanting to shine bright. A world where everyone aims to be the best version of themselves. Some may see this as naive, but I believe the possibilities are endless when we lean into faith love and a pure heart all of which stem from forgiving any human mistake you can think of.

I look back over my school years and I wasn't a very

happy child. I was always very socially awkward in my brown uniform. I remember the day sister Mercedes called my dad in in absolute disgust for it was appalling that I'd spilling slime all over my beautiful uniform. If only my dad had of told her what he really thought. The word beautiful and my uniform definitely didn't go. I don't know what lesson my sister was trying to teach me but if she was trying to instill cleanliness in me she did the opposite. Often I wonder why I found it so hard to keep myself clean and tidy but you can rest assured no matter how hard my mum or granny tried to dress me nice there was nothing could stop me from changing into "pockets" dresses which devasted my mum. We laugh about this now especially at Christmas time. We don't need cracker jokes in our house. My dad has a long list of reminiscing stories to tell about how I broke his heart, ha-ha.

It's taken me years to be able to reflect back on my family dramas and dilemmas in laughter. My dad couldn't ever wrap his head around how much I could take in school from people who'd be teasing me one week and they'd be down playing hopscotch the next, but I could stop talking to him for 2 years no problem.. I suppose it was a coping mechanism for me. It was easier to take my troubles out on my dad than it was to put up a fight with kids in school.

Fiánna-Jane changed our lives more than she could ever imagine. My granny said she gave her something to get up for in the mornings. My mum found love that she never had with her kids. She's the apple of my dad's eyes and her gg's (great grandparents) well they've a new lease of life.

I think the most important lesson Fiánna-Jane has taught us is it doesn't matter how the foundation of your life is built. There's no perfect to acknowledge all of the mistakes and hurdles you've faced where for a reason and finding a purpose for your life takes time to build. It's your story and you're wouldn't be handed a cross you can't bear. So forgive yourself for holding on to any part of what doesn't serve you. Rebuild that trust with the most important person in your life. You. The day you realise that number one relationship starts with you and forgiving yourself. Is the day you will be set free. As any mistake a person has made in your expense is a reflection on them and frankly none of your business. I say this at no offence but as a wake-up call. If we spent all our time focusing on trying to change others and how they treat us its time taken from doing nice things for ourselves. Fill your heart with days that set your soul on fire. Send love to others in hope that they do the same.

Love Sinéad

The Zone (Warrenpoint)

In March 2019, I had my first encounter with the IET Angels. My friends and I had booked an introduction to IET workshop with Jennifer Maddy a few weeks in advance. As the workshop date approached, I found myself looking for excuses to not go. For whatever reason I couldn't be bothered or muster the energy to attend. One of the friends in my group kept encouraging me though, insisting we must go. So on the day of the workshop I managed to get my act together and went to this friend's house while we waited…and waited…and waited for the other friend. She couldn't find the first friend's house and we were getting later and later for the workshop! She arrived finally, and eventually we made it to Jennifer's, a few hours late, nonetheless.

Jennifer was welcoming and accommodating regardless of our tardiness. We all got comfortable in her garden cabin and proceeded with the workshop.

One of the first things Jennifer said was that all our lives were about to change. In fact, the first friend I mentioned had been saying the same thing in the weeks and days leading up to the workshop. I think this is what eventually motivated me to attend. I had been sending out intentions recently to discover my purpose, my calling in life and hoped this may send some answers my way!

We carried on through the workshop for the day, then

exchanged personal stories, therapies and readings (as we are all in those fields) and ended up in HYSTERICS of laughter over silly anecdotes - heightened, no doubt, by the IET energy which had built up in the room over the day! What a pressure release!

I was glad I went, to say the least, if only for the craic we had!

Later, at home that evening, I found myself lost in thought for a moment wondering, again, about my life's mission or purpose. I "heard" in my head someone ask, "What do you really want to do?"

My IMMEDIATE answer (in my head) was: FOOD!

So that was it! I knew what I had to do!

Now I needed to find a place to do it! I had been playing with the idea of opening a small café with a small side room to do my therapies from, as I had been doing them from home and was considering expanding this practice. Periodically I had been checking local commercial property lets but never found anything suitable.

Well!! The NEXT DAY after the IET workshop I had the urge to do another property search and there it was!! …a property available for lease that I had NEVER seen before!

It was above and beyond anything I could have imagined! Not only did it have a front room suitable for a tearoom/café but there were 2 rooms suitable for use as therapy rooms!

It was also a fantastically beautiful seafront, Victorian-style building, full of character and as many who visit say, a wonderful energy!

Needless to say, I immediately contacted the agent, arranged a viewing and in time, it became The Zone Tearoom and Holistic Therapies!

It must be said too, that after having met a new circle of fellow therapists I was greatly confident this business would serve our professional community in many ways.

Also, greatly encouraged not only by my new friends (Jennifer included!), but through Mother Mary who I started connecting to during this time, I decided this venture should be dedicated to those whom Mary chose to send to me/us for assistance – especially women of the local community.

It is amazing to see the power of the energy we don't see with our human eyes come to fruition as we allow it to come through us.

I thank my new, but lifelong friends – Dymphna, Stephanie and Jennifer (among others) who led me to The Zone through the help of our Angel friends!

Love Paula xxx

We are Only Here to Help Others

To say these last few years have been hard would be an understatement. I was living in a house that had a small gas leak and was damp. Unbeknown to myself this was affecting my daughters Caitria and Sienna and my own health constant tonsillitis and infections stomach bugs. We could not breathe we struggled to awake in the mornings for school, the whole time it felt like I was constantly fighting an imaginary illness that I blamed on my anxiety and depression.

Over these last few years, I have studied psychology with counselling as my family have a history of different mental health diagnosis. I wanted to learn more about why these illnesses occurred and still continue to study and learn more to manage these symptoms and to help others. With everything that was going on I came across different people who I now consider to be very close friends that will always be in my life whether or not I see them all the time. I know I can contact them whatever the reason and likewise with themselves.

Throughout this mad journey I learnt that in actual fact I am a Psychic Medium- that I am not crazy and that what I was experiencing with life was in fact a great GIFT to help others.

I have taken many healing classes and have received a lot of certificates in completion of a range of Healing courses.

A friend of mine Dymphna introduced me to a lovely lady named Jenny Maddy. An amazing healer who teaches IET. We then arranged to go and do IET with Jenny and I brought my sister Mollie along who herself was going through life at a hard time. On the day we arrived in Dundalk we met Paula O'Hare another amazing psychic.

The moment we entered Jenny's house I could feel calmness in her lovely cabin in her garden, surrounded by green hills behind the hedges. The blue sky, breathing in fresh air on my face and in my lungs- her crystals scattered about the garden and when you walked in it was so cozy. Jenny had a lovely heated fire on. Jenny explained everything so clearly and the energy was amazing. The Angels, the healing, everything especially with the other ladies there. What a fantastic day! Jenny had gotten us to write down what we wanted to change in our lives and which Angels to ask to help us. We all had something to eat and had a fantastic day. So Mollie and I left to head back to Newry so relaxed and energetic talking about life and how Jenny and IET felt and looking forward to the future.

On the way home, Mollie asked for a sign from her Angels. We saw a man walking by the shopping centre holding his head speaking to himself and screaming in pain he fell to the ground. I shouted to Mollie, ' quick get out,' she did. I pulled the car over beside traffic lights put my hazards on and rang an ambulance. The police came and the man got the help he needed. After we got back in the car I said to Mollie,' you asked for a sign- we are here to help others'. There is definitely more for us on earth to do.' Afterwards we headed back to Belfast where a lot of other significant events happened, and we knew our Angels where helping us.

I soon discovered I was pregnant. Shortly after that I got news of another two bedroom house to rent, although it is not what I want for my future, it was a roof over our heads at a very difficult time and now we have Alayah who definitely is a little miracle. She has brought so much happiness to all of us!

I know where we are at the minute is helping heal my own family and myself and God is preparing us for our future, with the help of my Angels.

I am especially thankful to Jenny. She brought me so much comfort and peace. I love IET and use it to heal friends and family. I do know we shall see each other again soon- as the title suggests," We never say goodbye" so I'll just say see you later xxx

Love Stephanie Osborne xxx

Archangel Michael; The Main Man

I started meditation classed and loved them. In my mind's eye, I would see colour and shapes and this fascinated me. I went on to do Reiki 1, 2 and Master's which helped me develop more. I just fell in love with Archangel Michael. I could feel his strength and power within me and around me. I was in awe of his presence and thought "Why me". With his power and strength and messages with me, I remember thinking "Why not me"

With a lot of Soul searching and thinking "Why am I here, what's my lesson to learn in my life?" the answer I got was unconditional love for me and others. This took years of practice and many a time I would get upset and give out to Archangel Michael. But he was always smiling at me. His message to me was (IT IS SAFE FOR YOU TO LOVE).

When I was a child of 12 years of age, I dreamed of being a Nurse, but thought I wasn't clever enough, I'd never pass the exams. I did my leaving cert with this dream in mind. I remember applying to the CAO to do Nursing and praying, I would get in. I asked specifically to the Angels, Ancestor Guides to support and help me through the 4 years of study. My sons at the time were young boys and needed their mam, but their love and support was just unbelievable. So proud of them. I truly believe that the Angels were minding me. Needless to say, the exams were very hard, I struggled and nearly give up a few times, but believing in the Angels helped me so much. To this day, I still practice nursing.

I love my Angel Cards and I connect with them every day. Through my journey, I discovered I am Claircognizant and clairvoyant. Working with Spirit can be daunting sometimes. The messages can be like a jigsaw puzzle sometimes or very clear. I read for people and cast spells of Hope. I love when people come to me for a reading and I look in their eyes and read their Soul. What gives me passion and joy is when their eyes change and they are smiling. I know I have given hope. I read from a pure heart and love unconditionally. I have met some amazing Healers through my journey, whom I now call good friends.

The Angels have also thought me to my sense of humour. I have a wicked sense of humour sometimes. This keeps me grounded. Laughter is the medicine of the Soul.

Another miracle in my life, Love you Alex,

Love Granny Franny. xxx

ANGEL BLESSINGS

Hi, my name is Brenda Coburn Murnaghan from Pure Reflections in Dundalk, Ireland.

My journey started when my mum passed into Spirit in January 2011. She reawakened in me what I had blocked when I was a child. I would go to bed at night and I would see shapes appearing and moving from the pattern in the curtains. I used to look at them and I remember one night I put my head under the covers of my bed and that was it, I don't think it happened again.

So fast forward to 2011. I started to smell the scent of roses when I would go upstairs, my mum loved roses and has lots growing around the house and for some reason that is all I would place on her grave. Then out of the blue I went and attended a Reiki course. Since Reiki my mind, spirit and energy was changing. I started to see numbers, words and faces in the clouds when I would look up into the sky.

One day I was in my bedroom looking out the window and the clouds started moving and shapes forming, I stood there, and I could see exactly what happened when my mum passed. Every day I would see more and more it was so exciting, my bedroom became alive at night, so many different things started to happen. I had a box that appeared in front of me. It was like a gift with a bow. It was that close to me, I tried to touch it. It disappeared.

There were cartoon characters getting into cars and driving off into the countryside, in another corner of the room I would see charts like planet positions. There was one time I was sick not well at all and my bedroom ceiling was illuminated in the colours of the rainbow and I know now that it was the healing Angels working on me. Pictures would appear and seemed to be jumping / dancing on the bedroom walls. One night I had what seemed to be a projection of light come from one side of my room right over to the other side were a man was standing as if he was a lecturer in front of hundreds of people.

On another occasion I had hurt my finger during the day. I was feeding two stray cats. They just started coming into my back garden and would jump up on a roof what was then a shed. They would lie there watching in the kitchen window. So I started feeding them and eventually they came up on the kitchen window. This particular day one was sitting on the windowsill and I started to open the window, I had some bacon in my hand. As I got the window open and went to put the bacon on the sill the cat pawed really quickly to get it out of my hand, but she caught my finger and I pulled back really quickly. I wasn't cut or anything just really painful and started to throb and it got very swollen. I couldn't bend it. I ran it under the cold tap to cool it down. It was sore for the rest of the day. That night I went to bed all excited. I was calling it my sleepover with the Angels. My daughters were having a dance school sleep-over. I was nervous for them and hoped all would be ok, that their pupils would have a great time and nothing that shouldn't happen, would happen. So up to bed I went and started talking to my Angels as I normally would. Had a few of what I would now call normal things happen. Then I didn't feel so well. I started to feel sick, weak and had a clearing. I was worried as I had said to my daughter, if she needed me during the night to call and I would be with her in five minutes, she wasn't that far away. All that was going on in my head was what if she needed me. I couldn't drive the car; I wasn't fit to drive over to her. I kept talking to the Angels asking for healing for my finger and that everything be fine with Stacey my eldest daughter, that nothing would happen with her pupils during the sleepover. When all of a sudden on my ceiling words started to appear. "Use your own Energy, Stacey knows what to do, everything will be alright".

I thanked them for the message, it calmed me down and then I started to focus on my finger. I called in AA Raphael to help heal my finger, whilst visualising a green light flowing through my finger while holding my hand over it. The healing started to ease the pain and eventually I fell asleep. The next morning it wasn't as sore, and I could bend it a little. I went over to the dance studio where the sleepover was to help with the breakfast and hoping they all had a great time. Yes, it went perfectly just as I was told "Stacey knows what to do ".

I thanked the Angels and kept on thanking them.

Every day I wake up thanking them for being with me during the night and for the day that's is just beginning. This is only a portion of what the Angels and I experienced together so far and I have my mum to thank for bringing me back to them and opening me up to be a Holistic Healer offering various energy healing therapies…. Reiki, Tameana Celestial Healing, Rahanni Celestial Healing, Integrated Energy Therapy, Tuning Forks, Sound Healing and Universal Reflexology. I love working with each and every one of them. Just like Jennifer, I am a Grand Reiki Master.

My grandchildren love the Sound Healing. When they call in to visit me, they say nanny can we play the gongs and bowls. They just love it. I give them a wee sound Bath and they then give me one.

When Toby was born, he had an issue with reflux, so I would place the singing bowls around him and gently play them. He would always be smiling and gurgling with them. The minuet he would see the bowls being placed around him; he would get so excited. Afterwards he would be so calm and relaxed, and it seemed to help with the reflux. Allie would come and lie down beside hum and after I was finished, she would start playing the bowls. She was only three years old now she is seven and Toby is five. They just love it. The sound rebalances the whole body, the chakra system, and the auric field. The sound and vibrations work through your whole body, all you have to do is lie down relax and allow the sound to immerse your whole being. You can do this through a group Sound bath or a private one to one, where it is focused on the individual person.

Tuning Forks again a Sound instrument is another relaxing vibrational treatment which is great for stressed muscles, pains, stiffness in the body and more.

We all need self-care to keep ourselves going to get us through the week. Using all the types of energy healings, trying different ones out to see which ones you are drawn to. Which one works for you. Everyone is individual and we all have our own individual needs. There are lots to choose from, so enjoy trying them out to see which one suits you best.

I will end by saying the words as in the song by The Beatles "All we need is Love, Love is all we need"

Namaste

And many Angel Blessings, Brenda x

I would like to share this GUARDIAN ANGEL PRAYER by Martin O'Neill, another Master Instructor in IET, whom I met when doing our masters together in Derry with Edmond Carroll.

It connects me to my Daddy, Denis Maddy in Spirit. Always in my Heart, Love you. Jen.

by Edmond Carroll and Gretta Murphy, IET Master Instructor Trainers

In the dark of night, I will take your hand and hold you close to me,

When your eyes are sad and teardrops fall, I will kiss them so you see,

When you need someone to talk to, I will be by your side,

If troubles cloud your Soul, I will be your Guide,

In all these things you have to Trust,

and in your Heart you Know,

Guardian Angels, always Love You,

And Never let you Go.

*by **Martin O'Neill, IET Master Instructor***

I AM ONLY HERE TO BE TRUELY HELPFUL,

I AM HERE TO REPRESENT HIM, WHO SENT ME,

I DO NOT HAVE TO WORRY, ABOUT WHAT TO SAY OR DO,

AS, HE WHO SENT ME, WILL DIRECT ME.

I WILL BE WHEREEVER, HE WISHES, KNOWING HE GOES THERE WITH ME,

I AM HEALED, AS I ALLOW HIM TO TEACH ME TO HEAL.

Abstract from a Course in Miracles *by Helen Schucman.*

This abstract was given to me on my own healing journey

from Cancer by Ronan Dolan. The words resonate with my Soul and Today I say this Prayer asking God to Guide Me. Ronan also advised me to visualise Chemo as the "Blood of Christ running through my Veins." This visualisation has helped heal my body, mind and Soul during that time. I believe in the Christ Consciousness. We are Love. Share your Love.

I now teach this Healing Modality of the 'Christ Consciousness' to help people evolve to a higher state of being, especially for meditation and opening the gateway to Enlightenment.

Love Jen xxx

QUANTUM SHIFT IN CONSCIOUSNESS

I first came across Quantum Touch on the Internet in 2004. while doing a search for alternative methods of treating scoliosis instead of surgery. My wife Teresa had scoliosis as I had myself, although Teresa was a lot worse than me. Teresa had polio at the age of two in the 1950's. Teresa's right leg is shorter than the left leg which was causing scoliosis. I tried a couple of healing modalities for her aches and pains without success. When I came across the Quantum Touch Website, I had difficulty believing the information on the website stating that with a light touch bones will melt back into alignment. There were Doctors and Chiropractors on the website endorsing Quantum touch even with that and the fact that I was searching for something different, I still got it hard to swallow, and closed down the website. It wasn't until the next day, my curiosity got the better of me. I discovered that there was nobody doing Quantum Touch in Ireland.

I decided to take a chance, so I bought their book and videos. When I received them, I discovered that it took two or three people to get it going. Teresa said that it was my baby. I managed to get it going with some determination. The first time, I tried it out on Teresa, she had a pain in her neck, I tried it out with my fingertips. Teresa felt the energy and I could feel the energy coming from my fingertips. Teresa's pain went away. I was very happy and so was Teresa. I made my mind up then to become a practitioner. I became the first Quantum Touch Instructor in Ireland. Quantum touch can heal many conditions from Migraine, muscle pain, stress, depression, vertigo, back pain, fibromyalgia and much more. I have a background in farming, which I have moved on from.

James Laverty xx

I believe we are going through a Quantum Shift in Consciousness. An Awakening. Coming into alignment with our own Source Light Energy. Through James becoming a Quantum touch practitioner, he has also helped improve his wife's health. Teresa's Doctors are truly amazed with her condition from Polio. She is truly amazing and an inspirational lady. I met James and Teresa a few years ago when I moved into their estate in Haggardstown, in Dundalk. We connected straight away. James invited me around for a Healing.

In his healing room, I discovered that we both had a lot in common. I had studied Ki-Energy Massage in Dublin with my Pal Lisa from a previous chapter. James is also a practitioner in Ki-Energy. James uses the same crystals as well, that have the same energy as the Pyramid that I have in my Healing Room. It was such a relief to meet someone who had been attracted to learn the same courses as myself. James was delighted to connect to the Healing Angels of IET and completed his Basic and Intermediate Levels. He has such a strong healing gift and sends out Distant Healing to anyone who needs Healing, as I do too.

Because of my journey through Cancer, James became a volunteer in the Cara Cancer Support Centre in Dundalk, A foundation that is close to my Heart. He gives his time to do Energy Treatments with anyone who needs help.

When you are an Energy Healer, it is very important that you take time to clear your own energy field and look after your own Body, Mind and Soul. You can't heal from a cup that is empty. I treat myself monthly to a Ki Energy massage with a Lady called Margaret Murtagh who works in Life Gym on Anne Street, in Dundalk and other therapies when I feel my energy levels dropping. After receiving a treatment, I feel clearer, more relaxed, tuned in and ready to Heal the World.

Love Jen xxx

Advice from Maria Sabina, Mexican Healer and Poet

Heal yourself with the Light of the Sun and the rays of the Moon. With the sound of the river and the waterfall. With the swaying of the sea and the fluttering of birds. Heal yourself with mint, neem, and eucalyptus. Sweeten with lavender, rosemary and chamomile. Hug yourself with the cocoa bean and a hint of cinnamon. Put Love in tea instead of sugar and drink it looking at the stars. Heal yourself with the kisses that the wind gives you and the hugs of the rain. Stand strong with your bare feet on the ground and with everything that comes with it. Be smarter everyday by listening to your intuition, looking at the world with your forehead.

Jump, dance, sing, so that you live happier. Heal yourself, with beautiful love, and always remember...

You are the MEDICINE.

We never say goodbye,
for we know it's not the end.
Up above you went back home,
as we all must do some day.
Sometimes I look up to you and
shed a silent tear,
then in my mind,
I see your face and
free from pain you are.
We know your all around us,
and what a comfort that is.

WE NEVER SAY GOODBYE,
IT'S ONLY
TILL WE MEET AGAIN.

Grace Maddy